Between Bookends

Samantha N. Chencharik

BookLeaf Publishing

Presentation by *BookLeaf Publishing*

Web: www.bookleafpub.com

E-mail: info@bookleafpub.com

ISBN: 9789357210379

First edition 2022

DEDICATION

"Every blade of grass has its angel that bends over it and whispers, 'Grow, grow.'"

I am a field of gratitude —

To my husband, for being my first reader, my home, my unwavering partner, and the most loving father to our children here and in heaven. To my strong and selfless mother, supportive father, and extraordinary grandparents for giving me my first journals, books, and gentle nudges into writing. To Brittany, my forever sister, for being the greatest friend and example I could ever ask for as we grew into adulthood together.

A Burst of Soft Commotion

I exhale
Slowly
As another wave of nausea
Ripples through my sleepless body.

I curl forward
In my tangled duvet
Hot and motionless
My hand rests on my rounding belly.

I widen my eyes
A nudge moves beneath my palm
Soft and sudden
Shattering my solitude forever.

I bite my lip
As the flicker of you
Bursts into my night
Announcing your life in the in between.

I stare at the shadows on the ceiling
My face opens into a toothy smile
Tears slip down my cheeks
Catching in the creases of my dimples.

I hold my breath

Afraid to break the spell
But I laugh at our meeting,
This breathtaking beginning.

You are here,
I hold myself.
You are here,
I hold us.

I Will Tell Her

I will tell her
Birth is painful
But remind her
Of her strength
So powerful
It'll leave her breathless
As she watches her baby
Take their first breath.

I will tell her
One night
They're cocooned in your arms
But remind her
The next morning
They'll walk away on wobbly legs
Leaving versions of themselves
Behind for you to mourn.

I will tell her
About that first smile
But remind her
The laugh is soon to follow
And it will save her
And it will cage her
as she loses herself

in motherhood.

One day
She'll find herself alone again, I'll promise
And it will feel like her heart
has wandered away into the world.
She'll ask me
if it'll always feel like that.
I will tell her
I don't know yet.

Only
I won't
tell her any of this.
She must discover it for herself
Alone and aching
Like we all do.

I will simply tell her
She is enough.

Thinking About Your Kneecaps

I read somewhere
You are born without
Your knees
Missing boned babies

How old are we
When we learn
To kneel
To heal
Heel

I see you
Sitting on your knees
Playing without boundaries
Tendons binding
Grinding
Pain subsiding

Kneecaps
Hub caps
Little chocolate Sno-Caps
Sweet tooth
Cavities
Bone on bone

Gravity

The Stork

Deep into your crib I stood staring
Long I waited there,
Wondering,
Fearing,
Doubting,
Dreaming,
I ever dared to love before
But you lay there calling
And the world gave no sign
And the only sound there spoken
Was my whispered, shh
This I whispered
And midnight
Murmured back, shh
Merely this
a quiet coo
and nothing more.

I Promise You Not Forever

I'm sorry
For all the madness
All the fallbacks
All the fails.

For all the times
I didn't tell you
I love you
because I was
too exhausted
to exhale.

I'm sorry
for the gas
I hid beneath the covers
even though
we promised
to keep living
like young lovers.

I'm sorry
I kept track
of who changed
the most diapers

who fed
the most bottles
who snuck in
the most naps.

This isn't our forever
just our
beautiful,
chaotic
present
and it doesn't come
with any maps.

This
is the hard part,
when we rush
and we hide
and collide
through life,
and try to
remember
the why of each day.

The part
when we grow
and we crawl
and we pray
To be enough
For

Each other,
For
Him.

First Year of You

It's delicate,
this season.
Everything
is blanketed with a gentleness
as we move lightly
and lovingly around you.
A soft sway at nap time,
a quiet coo in the night,
a little hand brushing my arm
as I nurse you to sleep.

I've memorized you by now
Every movement you make
Every sweet howl you sing
Your mirroring smile
The way you giggle with glee.

Holding you now
I close my eyes
Tight
Trying desperately
to embed in my memory
the weight
and feel
of your entire body in my arms.

But I know
Any day now,
We will watch you
move with a quickness,
a sudden burst —
Shattering this stage
to make way for the next,
Another chrysalis.

Today, on your birthday,
My hand moves to my belly,
My eyes well with the memory
of all of your firsts
and all of those firsts
that turned into all of your lasts.
And I am so thankful
We were there
to watch them all unfold —
In this beautiful,
Breathtaking,
First year of you.

The Seamstress

I winced
As I wove
His little life
Into the tapestry
of her death.

The memory
Shakes
the needle in my hand
Knowing as his days grew
Hers began to shorten.

Stitch after stitch
Day after day
Brought me closer
to the impossible conclusion
that our time here is a fragile spool of thread.

I could suffocate in
This blanket of memories
Or use it to warm myself
In the years I will live without her.

My Bookends

I live in the endless memories of her
that steal me suddenly as
I nurse you in the night
or fold your tiny clothes
or rock you softly to sleep.
Or not so suddenly at all,
when the tears slip quietly into my day
and hold me hostage for the afternoon.

I live with your birth in my heart
and the birth of every baby to follow,
as the unwavering reminder
that life is meant to be lived
and loved —
that there is always a reason to hope.
that somehow
joy does come in the morning.

That we can hold joy and grief
in the fist of our hearts
at the same time.

That I can love
and lose

at the very same time.

That even though birth and death
look like untouchable bookends,
we all live the same in between:

holding onto hope
in search of joy
with the ones we love.

The Dig

Grief is an excavation of the heart.
The physical pain of your body
Preparing a new place
To keep this person
Sears through you
As a shovel of sorrow
Digs into your chest
Day after day.

But the hole will never be deep enough
To keep a memory as big as hers.
So you keep digging.
And along the way you find
The laughter you shared,
The tears you wiped away,
The plans you promised
One another.
And you remember
Just how wonderful
it really was.

Suddenly,
There, in the darkness
Of the hole you dug so deep

You realize
You can look up,
Look up
And see the light.

Giving Birth to Mourning

My funeral outfit
did not fit
my swollen postpartum belly.
Pressed against my dress pants
my bra straps dug into
my shoulders
heavy breasts
begged.
My bra soaked with milk
As I cried in the pew.

The priest's
foreign words
ping
ponged
in my head.
I couldn't hear him over the
Rattling inside of me.
My heart
shaking
like an empty spray paint can.

I looked up.
Where,
I wondered,

are you;
the strong woman
who loved and laughed for
thirty years,
two months,
and three short weeks.
One-hundred days shy
of your wedding day.
My eyes scanned the long aisle
you were supposed to walk down.

I escaped
Outside,
where I stood very still
on the cold church steps
staring
over the sea of people
who came for you
staring
at the tops
of Brooklyn's buildings.
My eyes lost,
trapped,
between earth
and sky.

Let Me Live in Your Desert

It is too quiet
And dry inside

I am learning
How to watch the rain
Without you
As the rhythm
Of a thousand pounds of water
Drowns you out
And floods me
With your absence

Here,
Under
Your
Roof,
There is only
Desert.

Sailing Away

My mind is tangled
Lost in a blanket of
Time and white caps
I lick my shivering lips
The dry wetness
On my tongue
On my skin
In the groves
of my shriveled fingertips —
Brining me.

My shuttered eyes are anchors
As the current cradles me
Softly at first
Then violently.
Dizzy
and desperate
I beg an empty sky.
Canvas
caresses my shoulder
I shudder and

leap,
Landing barefoot
on the tile

of our bathroom floor.

Flawed Valves

The heart is
A cliché
Set up for some
child's play

Beating
Fighting
Master
of our dying

60, 70, 80
Keep your hands
steady
90, 100

Are you having fun yet
Deep breath
Quick legs
Run until your body begs

For sleep
For rest
Your broken heart
Never knew what's best

This Happens Every Night

I'm not going anywhere,
I scream
into the silence
between us
as you fall asleep.

Your heavy eyelids hold me together.
I wish I could tell you another story
about Her,
But I won't wake you
Again.

I stare into the darkness
of our railroad apartment,
Drowning
in the echoes
inside my head.

I turn to face the wall,
The ruffles of the blanket
Threaten our shared solitude.
Afraid to break the spell,
I hold my breath and decide.

You will not find me

Where you left me,
I whisper.

I do not lay
where I fall.

The Epitaph Here

You swung
The city rose up
To meet you
Crushed and purple
You walked
Under the roads you chose.
There,
You wondered why
The underbelly
Of your heart was
Soft
But tongue
Sharp.
I shook my head
And held you tightly
You cried
I cried
It was as if the two years folded
Into one
And if I looked hard enough
Over the memory of your shoulder
I could find you standing
between the old headstones
Smiling at me
Like last November.

White Caps

I've always wanted to see
If I could survive
The storm of me.
To crash
into the shores of my life
To sail against the current
of myself.

Drift farther
Until the island is a speck
Rise to every high tide
Float on every calm wave.

Swim lessons taught me nothing.
The most dangerous of us
lack the fear of drowning.

Knife Block Alphabet

I swallow knives as night
You wake
Complaining
your throat hurts

The words
Shackled and shadowed
Consonances
vibrating my voice box

Vowels
quivering on my lips
My tongue
wrestles them
My uvula
Dances

One
By
One
I devour them whole
Until I
Choke

Bloody Cuticles

I bite my nails
I break my own heart
I burn bridges with beautiful views
Where do I start?

I spend every dollar bill that I've ever made
I don't stop when I feel the memories start to fade
I slash my own wrists for expensive blush
I like when you yell when we're in a rush.

I love like it's the first time I've been alive
Where there's nowhere to run
There's nowhere to hide.
I look at you now and I know it's not clear,

I'm a thousand broken things
but it'll all disappear.

Dry Ink

The sun is setting
The sailboats are in clusters
Far out past the buoys
The beach is a picture already painted,
A photograph already developed.

And though I can feel the sand underneath my
feet
And the salt on my lips,
It has already been.

Wind has already brushed through my hair,
The end of the shoreline has already come and
gone.
My riled eyes now lost in the division
Between where high tides began and
The setting sun disappeared
At the world's end.

The boats already docked
And the sailors already asleep.
And the red, red sunrise already burst
Into the crease of the darkness.

I followed it to the beginning of all things.

And there is where I found you
Already in love.

Two Places

All my life
I thought I needed calming seas,
Protective mountains,
Or those brilliant city lights.

How wrong was I.
All my life
I have sought you
Blindly.

Without knowing
Why
or when
or how
I would find you.

One day
You
Looked at me
and I knew.

All my life
I have existed in two places:
Where I am
And where you are.

Why Love

Love is the why of life,
It is the only reason we are here.

Love is why you eat my cooking
and say it's good.
Love is why you forgive me when I'm late
even though I know you hate it.
Love is why I don't mind when I wake up
to find you've stolen all the covers.
Love is why I read my favorite lines from books
to you
and love is why you always listen.

Love is why we can make a game out of
anything.
Love is why we stay up late
with a bottle of wine on the floor
and the windows wide open on a summer night.
Love is why we imagine our future together
like two teenagers who run away in the middle
of the night.
Love is why you hold me when it's hardest
and cradle me when I need it most.

Love is why we can still hold on
in the in-between.

www.ingramcontent.com/pod-product-compliance
Lightning Source LLC
Chambersburg PA
CBHW051750130826
49812CB00033B/1078
* 9 7 8 9 3 5 7 2 1 0 3 7 9 *